Experiments

Upon the Word

by
Susan Luke

Covenant Communications, Inc.

97 98 99 00 01 02 03   10 9 8 7 6 5 4 3 2 1

*Experiments Upon the Word: Learning the Gospel
Through Fun & Easy Object Lessons*
Covenant Communications, Inc.
ISBN 1-55503-137-6

To my husband, Monty, and my children,
Chris, Kim, Corinne, Karalyn,
Ammon, Jesse, and McKay.

You're the best!

TABLE OF CONTENTS

INTRODUCTION

My own experience has shown me that no matter what the age of the students being taught, object lessons are of great value. Whether you're trying to hold the attention of the very young, keep teenagers awake, or teach a basic gospel principle to "seasoned" members by putting a new twist on it, object lessons get the job done. The more senses you can stimulate in a person, the greater the impact of the lesson being taught. Your students may not remember every lesson they hear, but you can bet they will remember every lesson they see. After one particular lesson, some of the teenagers in a class I was teaching were inspired to go home and present the same object lesson to their families. Now, that's a lesson they'll remember! As with anything, practice makes perfect. When you find an experiment that will help you get the point across, practice it at home until you get it just right. You want the experiment to be successful so that the lesson will be memorable. Many of the experiments in this book have more than one gospel application. You may even think of other gospel principles that can be taught with the various experiments. However you decide to use them, have fun experimenting upon the word!

ARMOR OF GOD

"Put on the whole armour of God, that ye may be able to stand against the wiles of the devil."   Ephesians 6:11

•THINGS YOU WILL NEED
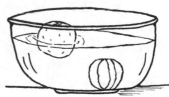

Two oranges
Bowl of water

•EXPERIMENT
Float the oranges in the bowl of water. Remove one of the oranges from the water and peel the skin away. Place the peeled orange into the water. It will now sink to the bottom of the bowl.

•GOSPEL APPLICATION
We learn from Ephesians 6:11-18 that we are to put on the whole armor of God, which includes truth, righteousness, peace, faith, salvation, and his word. When we put on the whole armor of God through righteous living and obedience to his commandments, we protect ourselves from the "fiery darts of the wicked." Just as the skin of the orange provides protection and gives the orange the ability to float atop the water, the armor of God gives us the ability to live above the wicked things of this world. Without its protection, we sink.

•ADDITIONAL APPLICATIONS

Temptation—The scriptures warn us several times not to give in to temptations. Satan and his followers would like nothing better than to deceive us and trick us into sin. As long as we live righteously, we have the strength to overpower him. This is demonstrated by the oranges floating on the water. But when we allow ourselves to be tempted by Satan, little by little he peels away our strength and protection. Eventually he has us in a completely weakened state—one where we sink into despair and hopelessness. This is demonstrated as you slowly peel away the skin of the orange. The orange could be placed into the water at different stages showing how Satan works on us a little at a time. Every time we give in, we allow ourselves to sink a little more. Eventually, all protection is peeled away and we are left to sink.

ASK OF GOD

"If any of you lack wisdom, let him ask of God...and it shall
be given him."   James 1:5

•THINGS YOU WILL NEED
Clear glass of water
An 8" piece of string
Salt shaker
Ice cube

•EXPERIMENT
Place the ice cube in the glass of water and have a
volunteer come forward and use the string to try
and lift the ice cube from the water. After the
volunteer gives up, wet the end of the string with
water and lay it on top of the ice cube. Sprinkle
salt on top of the string as well as the area around
it. After waiting a minute or so, the string will
freeze to the ice cube and you will be able to lift it
from the water.

•GOSPEL APPLICATION
Discuss with the class that some problems we face
in life are hard to solve on our own. This is
demonstrated by challenging a class member to
come forward and try to remove the ice cube from
the water by using only the string. As the
volunteer is unsuccessfully trying different ways
to lift the ice cube from the water, explain that we

can try to solve the problems by ourselves, but will soon find that we are just wasting time. We need the assistance of our Heavenly Father. In James 1:5, we learn that if we are lacking in wisdom we can ask of God, in faith, and receive answers. Through prayer, we ask God to help us find answers to our problems. Wet the end of the string with water and place it on the ice cube. Sprinkle the salt on the string as well as the area around it. While you are waiting for the string to freeze to the ice cube, have the class turn to Hebrews 11:6. We learn from this scripture that "God...is a rewarder of them that diligently seek him." He will reward us with the answers we seek if we truly have faith in him. Demonstrate this by successfully lifting the ice cube from the water.

•ADDITIONAL APPLICATIONS

Endure unto the end—1 Nephi 13:37 states, "...and if they endure unto the end they shall be lifted up at the last day, and shall be saved in the everlasting kingdom of the Lamb." Have two or three volunteers come forward and give them each a string and a glass of water containing an ice cube. Ask them to try to remove the ice cube from the water by using the string. After they have tried unsuccessfully, tell them there is a way this can be done, but if they want to be successful, they need to endure to the end. Assign and read aloud the following scriptures: Matthew 5:13, Ezekiel 43:24, 3 Nephi 12:13, and D&C 101:39. Ask what all of the scriptures have in common. (Salt.)

Bring out the salt shaker and complete the experiment. After waiting a minute or so, have someone read 1 Nephi 13:37 aloud as your volunteers successfully lift their ice cubes from the water.

THE ATONEMENT

"If we walk in the light...the blood of Jesus Christ his Son
cleanseth us from all sin." 1 John 1:7

•THINGS YOU WILL NEED

Clear glass jar
1/4 cup vinegar
A pinch of salt
10 to 20 copper pennies
Steel nail
Scouring powder

•EXPERIMENT

Pour the vinegar and salt into the jar. Add the
pennies to the jar of vinegar and let stand for a
few minutes. Clean the iron nail with the
scouring powder and rinse thoroughly. Drop the
clean nail into the vinegar with the pennies and
let sit for about fifteen minutes while you
continue the lesson. When complete, the pennies
will be clean, and the nail will be covered with
copper.

•GOSPEL APPLICATION

We learn from 1 John 1:7 that through the blood
of Jesus Christ we can be cleansed from our sins.
The tarnished pennies represent our unrepen-
tant state. The nail represents the suffering the
Savior endured to bring to pass atonement for

6

mankind. When we partake of the Atonement through sincere repentance (Mosiah 26:29-30), we can be cleansed and forgiven of our sins. Just as the nail took the tarnish from the pennies, Christ took upon himself the burden of our sins so that if we repent, we won't have to suffer for them.

BAPTISM

"Repent, and be baptized every one of you in the name of Jesus Christ for the remission of sins."   Acts 2:38

•THINGS YOU WILL NEED
Blotting paper (found in art supply stores)
Paper clip
Water
Two clear drinking glasses
Spoon
Sand

•EXPERIMENT
Make a filter from the blotting paper by cutting a circle that is approximately 5" in diameter. Make a straight cut from the outside of the circle to the center. Overlap the cut edges (forming a cone) and fasten with a paper clip. Set the filter aside. To begin the experiment, pour some clean water into one of the glasses. Place about one teaspoon of sand into the water and stir. Now place the cone filter in the other glass and slowly pour the sandy water through the filter. The sand should remain in the filter, leaving the water clean once again.

•GOSPEL APPLICATION
The fourth Article of Faith teaches us that after we have faith in Jesus Christ, we must repent and be

baptized by immersion for the remission of sins. Although each of us begins mortal life clean and pure, we will all make mistakes and therefore become unclean. Through sincere repentance and baptism by immersion, our sins can be "filtered" from our lives and we can become clean once more.

•ADDITIONAL APPLICATIONS

Clean living—Stir one teaspoon of sand into the water for each worldly influence the class can name. Some suggestions may be R-rated movies, immodest fashions, vulgar language, etc. The water becomes polluted and impure. Ask a volunteer if they would like a drink of the water. Of course not! But, how many of these wordly influences are we allowing to enter our minds and bodies each day? Pour the polluted water through the filter and into the clean glass. Just as we filter the sand from the water, we need to filter the bad of the world so that only the good influences us. We accomplish that by following God's commandments and counsel. If we follow the plan that God has given us, we will learn to "Set your affection on things above, not on things on the earth" (Colossians 3:2).

BEAR ONE ANOTHER'S BURDENS

"Bear ye one another's burdens, and so fulfil the law of Christ."
Galations 6:2

•THINGS YOU WILL NEED
Backpack
Several large rocks
Permanent ink marker

•EXPERIMENT
Using a permanent ink marker prior to the experiment, label each rock with a different burden that might be faced in life. Place the rocks into the pack to be carried by one person. The load will be extremely heavy. Take the rocks from the pack one at a time and distribute them to others. The load is then easier to bear.

•GOSPEL APPLICATION
Place the rocks into the pack one at a time as you discuss with the class each burden. When the pack is full, ask for a volunteer to come forward to carry the pack. Invite someone to read aloud Mosiah 18:8. Alma taught that if we want to be called the people of God, we need to be "willing to bear one another's burdens, that they might be light." Remove the rocks from the pack one at a time and share them with other members of the class. When the load is shared, the burden is

much lighter and easier to bear.

•ADDITIONAL APPLICATIONS

Freedom through repentance—Using a permanent ink marker, label each rock with a different sin. (This can be done prior to your presentation or during class if you want the class members' input.) Invite someone to come forward and place the pack on their back. Place the rocks into the pack one at a time. Each sin (rock) makes the pack a little heavier. Soon the pack of "sins" is extremely heavy. Sin weighs us down, depresses us, and makes it hard for us to function mentally and spiritually. When we properly repent of our sins, we can once again enjoy the freedom of righteous living. (Refer to Alma 36:5-24 for a wonderful account of Alma's conversion and remission of sins.)

Shun the adversary—Satan likes to bring our spirits down by making us believe things about ourselves that just aren't true. We learn in D&C 50:2-3 that Satan and his followers are in this world to deceive and overthrow us. Any negative thought that comes into our mind is from Satan. In Alma 5:40 we learn that "whatsoever is good cometh from God, and whatsoever is evil cometh from the devil." Ask the class to list things that Satan tries to make us believe while you write each of them on a rock. Some examples might be "I'm discouraged," or "I'm worthless." Place the rocks into the pack and ask for a volunteer to come forward to carry the pack. Just as the

11

volunteer is weighed down by the pack of rocks, our spirits are weighed down when we listen to Satan. Through continual prayer we can conquer Satan and his followers. (D&C 10:5.) Remove the rocks from the pack so that the volunteer can feel the freedom that comes from shunning the adversary.

BEAR UP YOUR BURDENS

"Beareth all things, believeth all things, hopeth all things,
endureth all things." 1 Corinthians 13:7

•THINGS YOU WILL NEED
Balloon
Drinking straw
Tape
Heavy book

•EXPERIMENT
Stretch the balloon prior to the experiment. Insert
the straw into the neck of the balloon and secure
tightly with tape. Place the balloon under the
book. Blow air through the straw into the balloon
causing the book to be lifted up.

•GOSPEL APPLICATION
"My people must be tried in all things," the Lord
declared, "that they may be prepared to receive the
glory that I have for them, even the glory of Zion;
and he that will not bear chastisement is not
worthy of my kingdom" (D&C 136:31). In
Abraham 3:25-26, we learn that the main reason
for our mortal probation is to be tested and tried
with hardships and temptations. We cannot
escape the trials that exist for our learning. When
we are called upon to endure a trial, we should
pray that Heavenly Father will strengthen

us—that we may be lifted up and our shoulders be made strong to carry the weight of the trial. This is demonstrated when the air is blown through the straw and into the balloon, strengthening it and helping it to lift the heavy burden of the book.

CLEANSED THROUGH REPENTANCE

"Let us cleanse ourselves from all filthiness of the flesh and spirit, perfecting holiness in the fear of God."   2 Corinthians 7:1

•THINGS YOU WILL NEED
Saucer
Plastic spoon
Salt
Pepper
Wool cloth

•EXPERIMENT
Pour some salt and a little bit of pepper into the saucer. Mix them together with your finger. First place the plastic spoon over the salt and pepper—close to it but not touching. Nothing should happen. Next, rub the plastic spoon on the wool cloth. Hold the spoon over the salt and pepper again. This time the pepper should stick to the spoon. **Note:** If all the pepper does not leave the salt, shake the pepper that has collected on the spoon into another container and start over by rubbing the spoon again.

•GOSPEL APPLICATION
Through the atonement of Jesus Christ, we have the opportunity to be forgiven of our sins. To be truly forgiven takes effort on our part. Demonstrate this by having the pepper represent

sin. When nothing is done to the spoon, the pepper (sin) remains. When effort is made by correctly following the repentance process (namely recognition of sin, remorse, confession, restitution, and the desire to forsake the sin), we can be cleansed and made pure again. Demonstrate this by rubbing the spoon on the woolen cloth and holding the spoon just over the salt and pepper mixture.

ENTANGLE NOT IN SIN

"Entangle not yourselves in sin, but let your hands be clean,
until the Lord comes." D&C 88:86

•THINGS YOU WILL NEED
Rope or twine

•EXPERIMENT
After the unknotted rope is shown to the class, tie the rope into several knots—some tight, some loose. When the time is appropriate during the lesson, try to untie the knots.

•GOSPEL APPLICATION
Hold the rope for the class to see. This represents someone who is virtually free from sin. As a mistake is made, though, it's like tying a knot in our otherwise clean, untangled life. Some sins are more serious than others, just as some knots are tighter than others. In D&C 88:86, we are counseled to "entangle not yourselves in sin, but let your hands be clean, until the Lord comes." With some effort on our part, we can be forgiven of our sins through the atonement of Jesus Christ. Some sins take more time and effort to repent of, just like the tighter knots take more time and effort to untie compared to the loose knots. We should all strive to keep our lives untangled and free from sin.

•ADDITIONAL APPLICATIONS

Testimony—Testimonies are like knots in a rope. Some testimonies have been made strong by trials and tribulations—just as some knots are made strong by pulling and tugging at the ends of the rope to tighten and strengthen the knot. Some testimonies have not been tested and are weaker—just as some knots are loose from lack of opposition at each end of the rope. Just as it is harder to undo a tight knot compared to a loose knot, it is harder to "undo" a strong testimony compared to a weak one. If we were hanging by a rope over the edge of a cliff, we would want to be sure that the knots in the rope were strong enough to keep us from falling. We should have the same desire to make sure our testimony is strong enough to keep us from falling into the hands of the adversary.

EVEN BALANCE

"Let me be weighed in an even balance, that God may
know mine integrity."   Proverbs 31:6

•THINGS YOU WILL NEED
Hammer
A 10" piece of string
A 12" ruler

•EXPERIMENT
Tie the ends of the string together, forming a
simple loop. Place the loop around the ruler and
the handle of the hammer. Suspend the ruler
from the edge of the table as shown in the
illustration above. Adjust the string so that the
hammer and ruler are balanced and suspend from
the edge of the table without falling to the floor.
Note: Be careful when adjusting the string so that
the hammer doesn't fall on your toes!

•GOSPEL APPLICATION
Sometimes we get caught up in the desire to
attain worldly knowledge, riches, or pleasure. If
these are our only desires, we will become
unbalanced and be stopped in our progression
toward eternal salvation. In D&C 11:23, the Lord
counseled Hyrum Smith to "seek the kingdom of
God, and all things shall be added according to
that which is just." We should follow the same

counsel and put the gospel at the center of our lives. By doing so, we will have the proper balance and continue to progress toward exaltation. To demonstrate this, let the hammer and ruler represent worldly desires. When each item is suspended from the edge of the table by itself, it falls. The gospel is represented by the string. Place the string around the ruler and the handle of the hammer and suspend the ruler from the edge of a table. Adjust the string so that everything is balanced and able to suspend freely. (Refer to the illustration on page 19.)

•ADDITIONAL APPLICATIONS

Self-mastery—In Alma 38:12, Alma counseled his son, Shiblon, to "bridle all your passions." We also learn from Proverbs 25:28, "He that hath no rule over his own spirit is like a city that is broken down, and without walls." We cannot find true happiness when we are servants to uncontrollable passions and appetites. Our spirits are more powerful than our bodies, and Heavenly Father has promised us that we will not be "tempted above that ye are able" and that he will also "make a way to escape" (Corinthians 10:13). By gaining control over our passions, we will attain a balance in our lives that will help us reach exaltation. Demonstrate this by placing the loop of string around the ruler and the handle of the hammer. The ruler and the hammer represent worldly passions and appetites. The string represents self-mastery. Place the ruler at the edge of the table. When adjusted properly, the string prevents the ruler and hammer from becoming unbalanced and falling to the ground.

EXAMPLES

"Be thou an example of the believers, in word, in conversation, in charity, in spirit, in faith, in purity." 1 Timothy 4:12

•THINGS YOU WILL NEED
Leaves
A crayon
Paper

•EXPERIMENT
Place the paper on top of the leaf and rub over the leaf with the side of a crayon. The image of the leaf will transfer to the paper.

•GOSPEL APPLICATION
Just as Christ was an example to us, we need to be an example to others. In 1 Timothy 4:12 it states, "Let no man despise thy youth; but be thou an example of the believers, in word, in conversation, in charity, in spirit, in faith, in purity." Our good example can "rub off" on others and influence them to do good also. Demonstrate this by doing a rubbing of the leaf. Show how the leaf and the rubbing are alike. We must be watchful, however, because a bad example can rub off also. Demonstrate this by tearing away a part of another leaf (representing sin). Do a rubbing of the partial leaf. Compare the two rubbings. Each rubbing duplicates the image

of the leaf that was used. We must always strive to set good examples to those around us.

•ADDITIONAL APPLICATIONS

Created in God's image—We learn in Genesis 1:26 and in Moses 6:9 that we were created in the image of God. Demonstrate what it means to be in the image of something by doing several rubbings of various items such as leaves, flat lace, or embossed images. When compared, we can see the image of the original in each rubbing.

GOSSIPING

"Whoso keepeth his mouth and his tongue keepeth his
soul from troubles." Proverbs 21:23

•THINGS YOU WILL NEED
Blotting paper (found at art supply stores)—cut
into four narrow strips
Four different black ink pens
Shallow bowl or saucer
Water

•EXPERIMENT
Prior to the lesson, place one large dot of ink 1"
from one end of each strip of blotting paper. Use a
different marker for each strip. Place the dotted
end of each strip into the saucer of water. Let sit as
the water separates the ink in each dot.

•GOSPEL APPLICATION
We are commanded in Leviticus 19:16 not to be a
talebearer—or in other words, not to be one who
gossips. Spreading gossip is harmful because facts
are lost when stories are retold—giving an unfair
perception of the one who is the target of gossip.
In Proverbs 18:8 it says, "The words of a talebearer
are as wounds, and they go down into the
innermost parts of the belly." Good advice is
found in Proverbs 21:23 which states, "Whoso
keepeth his mouth and his tongue keepeth his

soul from troubles." In the demonstration, the black dots represent the same story being told to four different people. All four people hear the same story to begin with, but as they retell their version, some things might be added and some things might be omitted. This is demonstrated by the various ways the inks are separated by the water.

•ADDITIONAL APPLICATIONS

Talents—In D&C 46:11 we learn that each of us is given different gifts (or talents) by the Spirit of God. We also learn in Moroni 10:18,30 that these gifts come from Christ and that we should "lay hold upon every good gift." To demonstrate that each of us is individual and has been given different gifts, place the four strips in the saucer of water. As the ink separates, it represents the various gifts that are within each of us. Each dot of ink separates differently, just as each one of us posseses different talents. Some of us may not even realize the different talents that lie within us until we truly search, find, and exercise them.

HELPING OTHERS

"When ye are in the service of your fellow beings ye are only
in the service of your God." Mosiah 2:17

•THINGS YOU WILL NEED
Modeling clay (not play-doh™ or homemade
playdough)
Clear glass bowl filled with water

•EXPERIMENT
Begin by shaping four balls (three small and one
large) from the clay. Drop the balls of clay into the
bowl of water. Each one sinks to the bottom.
Remove the largest ball of clay and shape it into a
boat. Float it on top of the water. Retrieve the
other balls and place them into the boat. The boat
supports itself and the other clay balls.

•GOSPEL APPLICATION
In Mosiah 18:8-9 we learn that part of our
commitment at baptism is to be willing to "bear
one another's burdens," "mourn with those that
mourn," and "comfort those that stand in need of
comfort." The three small balls of clay represent
three different people—one who is laden with
burdens, one who is mourning, and one who is in
need of comfort. Explain this to your class as you
drop each ball into the water. Roll the larger ball
of clay in your hands as you explain that if we are

all "rolled up" in ourselves, we will not be able to help those in need. Demonstrate this by dropping the larger ball of clay into the water also. Each ball sank. Remove the larger ball of clay from the water. Stretch and shape the clay into a small "boat"—symbolic of the stretching and shaping we need to do in our own lives in order to help others. We need to be flexible and giving and willing to help those around us. Place the clay boat into the water. Retrieve the smaller balls and place them into the boat to show how we can help support others in their times of need.

•ADDITIONAL APPLICATIONS

Strengthen thy brethren—In Luke 22:32 it states, "...and when thou art converted, strengthen thy brethren." The small balls of clay could represent nonmembers, new members, or less-active members who are not totally converted to the gospel of Jesus Christ. When dropped into the water, they sink. (Do not place the larger ball into the water.) The larger ball of clay represents someone who has been converted to the gospel of Jesus Christ. Read Luke 22:32 as you shape the clay into a small boat. Float the boat on the water. Place the balls of clay into the boat. This demonstrates that by "spreading" the gospel we can support and strengthen others who are not yet converted to the gospel of Jesus Christ.

HIDDEN SINS

"Ye cannot hide your crimes from God; and except ye repent they will stand as a testimony against you at the last day." Alma 39:8

•THINGS YOU WILL NEED
Two tablets of any laxative (not chocolate flavored) containing phenolphthalein
One tablespoon rubbing alcohol
Wet bar of <u>white</u> soap
Tub of water
Hand towel

•EXPERIMENT
Crush the two tablets into a fine powder and add the rubbing alcohol to form a paste. Rub the paste onto a volunteer's hands and let dry. Give the volunteer a wet bar of white soap. The chemical reaction of the laxative and soap should form the color of fuschia.

•GOSPEL APPLICATION
We may be able to hide our trangressions from those around us, but we can never hide our sins from Heavenly Father. In Alma 39:8 it states, "But behold, ye cannot hide your crimes from God; and except ye repent they will stand as a testimony against you at the last day." When we reach the end of our mortal existence, we will stand before God to be judged of him. If we are not clean, our

sins will be "as scarlet," not "white as snow" (Isaiah 1:18). The dried paste represents our hidden sins. Our sins may not be completely noticeable to those around us, but when we stand in front of the Lord to be judged (the wet bar of soap), our sins will be made known. **Note:** The paste could be placed on the hand of the teacher ahead of time so that the class is completely unaware of the "sins" until it is made known by the wet bar of soap.

•ADDITIONAL APPLICATIONS

Cleansed through the blood of Christ—We learn in Mosiah 4:2 that the people in King Benjamin's time cried unto the Lord for mercy. They desired forgiveness of their sins, and this was only possible through the atoning blood of Jesus Christ. In John 1:5, it states, "And from Jesus Christ, who is the faithful witness, and the first begotten of the dead, and the prince of the kings of the earth. Unto him that loved us, and washed us from our sins in his own blood." It is only through the blood of Christ that we can be washed from our sins. The dried paste represents sin. As the hands are washed with the soap, the "atoning blood" is revealed. Continue to wash with the soap until the hands are completely clean.

HIDDEN TREASURES

"All saints who...keep and do these sayings...shall find...great treasures of knowledge, even hidden treasures." D&C 89:18-19

• **THINGS YOU WILL NEED**
Several coins
Large opaque bowl
"Fun-Tack" or clear tape
Pitcher of water

• **EXPERIMENT**
Prior to the lesson, secure the coins to the inside bottom of the bowl with "Fun-Tack" or clear tape. During the lesson invite a volunteer to come forward and look over the edge of the bowl at the coins. Then ask the volunteer to move backward until they can no longer see the coins at the bottom of the bowl. Have them stay where they are standing. During the demonstration, slowly pour the water into the bowl a little at a time until the volunteer can see the coins again from where they are standing. **Note:** This optical illusion occurs when the bowl is full of water and the light bends so that your volunteer is able to see the reflection of the coins.

• **GOSPEL APPLICATION**
In D&C 89:18-19 we find a wonderful promise given by the Lord to all obedient saints. For those

who keep the Word of Wisdom, they "shall find wisdom and great treasures of knowledge, even hidden treasures." After your volunteer has moved backwards and is in a position where they can no longer see the coins, discuss the various "words of wisdom" given in section 89. With each principle discussed, pour a little bit of the water into the bowl—symbolizing obedience to the principle. Eventually, when the bowl is full of water, the volunteer's "obedience" will bring into view the great treasures of knowledge and wisdom (symbolized by the coins) that were once hidden from their sight.

HOLY GHOST

"And by the power of the Holy Ghost ye may know the truth of all things." Moroni 10:5

•THINGS YOU WILL NEED

Two paper cups
A 6'-8' piece of string
Two paper clips
5 blank envelopes

•EXPERIMENT

Using two cups, carefully poke a small hole in the bottom of each. Thread one end of the string through the bottom of one cup and tie the string to a paper clip. (The paper clip will be on the inside of the cup.) Thread the other end of the string through the bottom of the other cup and tie it to a paper clip in the same fashion. Set aside. Label each envelope with a word or phrase that describes something that would interfere with hearing the Holy Ghost such as SELFISHNESS, SIN, PRIDE, PREOCCUPATION WITH WORLDLY THINGS, etc. When the cups are held apart by two people, and the string is kept tight, they act as a line of communication with one person talking, and the other person listening. When the envelopes are hung on the line, there is interference and the message is almost impossible to hear.

32

•GOSPEL APPLICATION

We learn in D&C 85:6 that the Holy Ghost is "the still small voice, which whispereth through and pierceth all things." Through him we receive truth, comfort, and revelation from Heavenly Father. His voice can be as a whisper, and we need to be spiritually in tune to hear him. Demonstrate this by having someone hold one of the cups to their ear, and as you pull the string tight, speak softly into the other cup. Your voice will be carried along the string and will be heard by the other person. Point out that the string is free from interference and therefore can carry the message without interuption. Sometimes we are not in tune to the whisperings of the Spirit. Some of our choices and actions will cause interference. In Helaman 4:24, the Nephites found that their actions were preventing them from hearing the Spirit of the Lord. While the string is tight, have someone hang the flaps of the pre-labeled envelopes over the string. Speak softly again to the person while the envelopes hang on the string. Your voice will be nearly impossible to hear. Discuss how each thing would interfere with your hearing the Holy Ghost and why it is important to keep the line of communication open and free of interference.

•ADDITIONAL APPLICATIONS

Prayer—In Proverbs 15:29 it says, "The Lord is far from the wicked: but he heareth the prayer of the righteous." When we keep the lines of communication open between us and the Lord by righteous living, it is easier for our prayers to be heard and answered. Unrighteous acts cause interference and make it difficult to communicate with the Lord.

INTELLIGENCE

"Whatever principle of intelligence we attain unto in this life, it will rise with us in the resurrection." D&C 130:18

•THINGS YOU WILL NEED
Two balloons of equal size—one filled with helium, the other filled with air
Permanent ink marker
Scriptures

•EXPERIMENT
Prior to the start of class, use a permanent ink marker to carefully write the words KNOWLEDGE and INTELLIGENCE on the helium-filled balloon. Write the words MONEY, FAME, WORLDLY POSSESSIONS, etc. on the air-filled balloon. Attach both balloons to the table, or hold onto each, so that the class does not realize that the balloons are filled differently. When both balloons are released at the same time, the helium-filled balloon will rise, while the air-filled balloon will not.

•GOSPEL APPLICATION
In D&C 130:18-19, we learn that the knowledge and intelligence we obtain in this life will rise

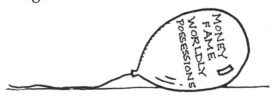

with us in the resurrection and benefit us in the world to come. To demonstrate this principle, release both balloons at the same time and watch as the helium-filled balloon rises and the air-filled balloon does not.

•ADDITIONAL APPLICATIONS

Second Coming of Christ—Prior to the lesson, place a picture of the Second Coming of Christ high on the classroom wall. In D&C 5:35 it states, "And if thou art faithful in keeping my commandments, thou shalt be lifted up at the last day." Prior to the start of class, use a permanent ink marker to carefully draw a happy face and the words FAITHFUL IN KEEPING THE COM-MANDMENTS on a white, helium-filled balloon. Draw a sad face and the words UNFAITHFUL IN KEEPING THE COMMANDMENTS on a black, air-filled balloon. (This can be done with a white paint pen.) Attach both balloons to the table, or hold onto each, so that the class does not realize the balloons are filled differently. Invite someone to read aloud D&C 5:35 as you release the balloons. The "faithful" balloon will rise up to meet the Savior, the "unfaithful" balloon fall to the ground. **Note:** You could carry this experiment one step further by referring to D&C 29:17 and destroying (popping) the "unfaithful" balloon.

LACK OF SPIRITUALITY

"For the Spirit of the Lord will not always strive with man."
2 Nephi 26:11

•THINGS YOU WILL NEED
Bowl
Ice cubes
Rice

•EXPERIMENT
Place the ice cubes into the bowl. Sprinkle some rice on the table next to the bowl. Invite a volunteer to come forward and place their hand in the bowl of ice for 30 seconds. Dry their hand and ask them to try picking up some of the grains of rice. Because their sense of touch has been dulled by the coldness, it will be hard to do.

•GOSPEL APPLICATION
Nephi warns us in 2 Nephi 26:11 that "the Spirit of the Lord will not always strive with man. And when the Spirit ceaseth to strive with man then cometh speedy destruction." As the volunteer places their hand into the ice cubes, discuss some of the various reasons the Spirit of God would cease to dwell with man. When we distance ourselves from spiritual things by putting off things such as church service, scripture study, etc., we become "cold" to the enlightenment of the

Spirit. For this experiment, the grains of rice represent bits of spiritual enlightenment given to us by the power of the Holy Ghost. When the Spirit is unable to dwell within us because of sin, slothfulness, contention, etc., it makes it difficult to gain spiritual bits of wisdom, knowledge, and understanding. Demonstrate this by having the volunteer try to pick up the grains of rice with their cold hand. This should be a difficult task. Fortunately, with some work, we can once again enjoy the influence of the Spirit by "warming" ourselves with prayer, scripture study, service to others, etc. Have the volunteer warm their hand by vigorously rubbing both hands together. Now, with a warm hand, they should be successful in picking up "spiritual bits of wisdom and knowledge."

LET YOUR LIGHT SHINE

"Let your light so shine before men, that they may see your good works, and glorify your Father which is in heaven." Matthew 5:16

•THINGS YOU WILL NEED

Clear plastic bottle
Pointed scissors
Water
Flashlight
Clear glass bowl

•EXPERIMENT

Set the bottle and bowl side by side on a table. With your scissors, carefully poke a hole in the bottle about an inch above the height of the bowl. Place your finger over the hole (or place duct tape over it) and fill the bottle with water. Place the bottle next to the bowl and have someone turn off the lights. Uncover the hole and shine the flashlight through the bottle as the water streams from the bottle and into the bowl. The brightness of the stream of water will vary depending on where you shine the flashlight. When the flashlight is positioned correctly, the water in the bowl should illuminate also.

•GOSPEL APPLICATION

While preaching the Sermon on the Mount, Jesus taught, "Let your light so shine before men, that they may see your good works, and glorify your Father which is in heaven" (Matthew 5:16). Jesus set the perfect example of good works for us to follow. In 3 Nephi 18:16 Christ told the Nephites, "Behold I am the light; I have set an example for you." If we have faith in him and follow his example, we will be "sure and steadfast, always abounding in good works, being led to glorify God" (Ether 12:4). Just as the light from the flashlight illuminates the stream of water and the water in the bowl, we can illuminate others as we follow the example of Jesus.

THE LOVE OF GOD

"The love of God, which sheddeth itself abroad in the hearts of
the children of men...is the most desirable above all things."
1 Nephi 11:22

•THINGS YOU WILL NEED
White frosting
Plastic spoons

•EXPERIMENT
Give each person a spoonful of frosting during
the lesson as you discuss the love of God.

•GOSPEL APPLICATION
Lehi's vision of the tree of life helps us to
understand the sweetness and beauty of the
gospel.   Lehi said, "And it came to pass that I
beheld a tree, whose fruit was desirable to make
one happy. And it came to pass that I did go forth
and partake of the fruit thereof; and I beheld that
it was most sweet, above all that I ever before
tasted" (1 Nephi 8:10-11). After he partook of the
fruit, his soul was filled with "exceedingly great
joy" and he was desirous for his family to partake
also. (1 Nephi 8:12.) In 1 Nephi 11:25, Nephi
learns that the tree of life represents the love of
God. The sweet, white frosting is symbolic of the
fruit that Lehi partook of in his dream. As Lehi
was desirous to share the fruit with his family,
share the frosting with the members of the class.

41

Encourage everyone to share the sweetness of the gospel with others so that they too can enjoy the sweetness of the love of God.

•ADDITIONAL APPLICATIONS

Spreading the Gospel—In this experiment you will also need small cookies or graham crackers, and a knife to spread the frosting. Pass out the cookies to the class members, but instruct them not to eat them yet. In Mosiah 3:20, King Benjamin foretold a time when the "knowledge of the Savior shall spread throughout every nation, kindred, tongue, and people." In order for this to happen, we need to do our part in spreading the gospel. As a class, discuss various ways of spreading the gospel. Joseph Smith once said, "We don't ask any people to throw away any good they have got; we only ask them to come and get more." (*History of the Church*, 5:259, Deseret Book Co., 1967.) The class members already have something good (the cookie). Now share more goodness with them by spreading the frosting (gospel) onto each cookie.

LOVE ONE ANOTHER

"Let us love one another: for love is of God; and every one that
loveth is born of God, and knoweth God." 1 John 4:7

•THINGS YOU WILL NEED
Clear drinking glass filled
with **one** cup of water
One fresh egg
Salt (about 1/4 cup)
Tablespoon
Permanent ink marker

•EXPERIMENT
Prior to the experiment, carefully draw a face on
the egg with a permanent ink marker (optional).
Place the egg in the glass of water to demonstrate
how it sinks to the bottom. Remove the egg and
stir in the salt, one tablespoon at a time. When all
the salt has been added, replace the egg to
demonstrate that it now floats.

•GOSPEL APPLICATION
Carefully place the egg into the water and explain
that the egg represents someone who is not
receiving love from others. It sinks to the bottom.
In John 15:12, we learn that it is a commandment
to love one another. Remove the egg from the
water and set it aside. Using one tablespoonful at
a time, stir the salt into the water as you mention

various ways to show love for others. Replace the egg to demonstrate how the egg is now supported with "love" and now floats instead of sinks. **Note:** This experiment could be used to demonstrate the need to show love to family members, ward members, neighbors, etc.

•ADDITIONAL APPLICATIONS

Goal setting— With so many things expected of us, it's easy to feel overwhelmed. Without proper objectives (goals), we can sink fast. (Carefully add the egg to the glass of water.) As we set goals and accomplish them, we find that we are better able to cope with our responsibilities. (Remove the egg and stir in a tablespoon of salt for each goal discussed. Replace the egg.) Eventually we are "floating" instead of "sinking." D&C 103:36 states, "All victory and glory is brought to pass unto you through your diligence, faithfulness, and prayers of faith." If we are diligent and faithful in our goals, then we will be victorious in our righteous desires.

MAGNIFY YOUR CALLING

"And we did magnify our office unto the Lord." Jacob 1:19

•THINGS YOU WILL NEED
Magnifying glass
Copy of quote listed below
Scriptures

•EXPERIMENT
The magnifying glass is used to enlarge the print of a quote so that it can be read aloud to the class.

•GOSPEL APPLICATION
In Jacob 1:18-19 we learn of the example that Jacob and his brother, Joseph, set in magnifying their callings. They taught the word of God with all diligence—laboring with all their might so that their garments would be found spotless at the last day. In the May 1986 issue of the *Ensign*, Thomas S. Monson told us what it means to magnify a calling. Have someone use the magnifying glass to read the quote below.

What does it mean to magnify a calling? It means to build it up in dignity and importance, to make it honorable and commendable in the eyes of all men, to enlarge and strengthen it, to let the light of heaven shine through it to the view of other men. And how does one magnify a calling? Simply by performing the service that pertains to it.

OUR BODIES ARE TEMPLES

"Know ye not that ye are the temple of God, and that the Spirit of God dwelleth in you?" 1 Corinthians 3:16

•THINGS YOU WILL NEED
Two clear glasses
Food coloring or ink
Two white carnations

•EXPERIMENT
The preparation for this experiment needs to take place several hours (or one day) before the presentation. Place about an inch of water into one glass. Add food coloring or ink to the water. Trim the stems of the flowers to about 6" in length. Place one of the flowers into the colored water and let it sit for several hours. Place the other flower into the glass with regular water. Set aside to be used during the presentation. As the first flower absorbs the colored water, the flower changes color.

•GOSPEL APPLICATION
We learn in 1 Corinthians 3:16 that our bodies are temples in which the Spirit of God dwells. With that being the case, we need to treat our bodies with respect and be careful what we subject them to. In D&C 89, the Lord revealed to Joseph Smith words of wisdom on how we should treat our

bodies. To show that what we put into our bodies does affect us, place the food color or ink into the glass of clear water. Point out that even though the flower is white at the moment, it will slowly absorb the colored water and be affected both internally and externally. This concept is demonstrated by showing the previously prepared flower to the class. If we follow the counsel given us in the Word of Wisdom, and are respectful of our bodies, great blessings will be ours (refer to D&C 89: 18-20).

•ADDITIONAL APPLICATIONS

Morality—The people and things in our lives, such as our friends, our hobbies, our choices of movies, books, magazines, TV shows, etc., can greatly affect us. Whether we realize it or not, our surroundings can influence us for good or evil. If we choose to associate with friends who are contentious, unkind, or immoral, then we stand a greater risk of becoming the same way. Every time we expose ourselves to wickedness, we can absorb some of it and be affected by it. Demonstrate this by showing the two flowers. The flower in the colored water represents someone who has chosen to be surrounded by (and therefore absorbing) unrighteousness. The flower in the clear water represents someone who has chosen to be surrounded by righteousness.

OUTWARD APPEARANCE

"For the Lord seeth not as a man seeth; for a man looketh on the outward appearance, but the Lord looketh on the heart."   1 Sam. 16:7

•THINGS YOU WILL NEED

Blue or green food coloring
A carton of milk
Paper cups
Cookies (optional)

•EXPERIMENT

Prior to the lesson, drop several drops of food coloring into the carton of milk and stir. Close the carton.

•GOSPEL APPLICATION

Offer cookies and milk to the class. (If you have a large class, you might ask for just a few class members to come forward and participate.) As you pour the milk into the cups, some members may not want to partake because of the unusual appearance of the milk—even though the milk's taste is not affected. We learn from 1 Samuel 16:7 that "man looketh on the outward appearance." If we want others to know that we are followers of Christ, then our appearance needs to reflect that—not only our outward appearance, but our words and actions also. When our appearance does not reflect Christ, then we will have a hard time converting others to his gospel. Just as the appearance of the milk might discourage some participants from tasting it, the wrong outward appearance could discourage some people from accepting the truthfulness of the gospel.

•ADDITIONAL APPLICATIONS

Judging others—Offer several classmembers a glass of milk. As you pour it, some members may not be so eager to drink it. They may pre-judge the taste by its appearance. When it comes to judging others, we are warned in Moroni 7:18 to "not judge wrongfully; for with that same judgment which ye judge ye shall also be judged." We need to follow the example of the Lord in 1 Samuel 16:7, who "looketh on the heart" of the individual. Since we do not have the ability to see a person's heart in the way the Lord does, we need to do all we can to get to know someone before we offer up judgment—and then only with "righteous judgment" as stated in John 7:24.

(OVERCOMING THE WORLD)

"He that is faithful and endureth shall overcome the world."
D&C 63:47

•THINGS YOU WILL NEED
Ping pong ball
Glass quart jar with lid
Wheat (to fill the jar)
Permanent ink marker

•EXPERIMENT
Using a permanent marker, draw a face on the ping pong ball. Place the ball into the jar. Fill the jar within 11/2" of the top with wheat. Place the lid on the jar and tighten. Turn the jar upside down and gently shake until the ping pong ball comes to the surface.

•GOSPEL APPLICATION
In John 16:33, Christ teaches us that we will have tribulations in this world. Place the ball into the jar and discuss various tribulations we may face. As each is mentioned, place a scoop of wheat on top of the ball. Continue until the ball is completely covered and the jar is filled to within 11/2" of the top. Place the lid on the jar and tighten. We also learn from the same scripture that we should be of good cheer because Christ overcame the world. If we are faithful and

50

endure, we shall also overcome the world. (D&C 63:47.) Turn the jar over and gently shake until the ball "overcomes" the wheat.

•ADDITIONAL APPLICATIONS

Goal setting—Many of the goals we set in life are not accomplished by one or two simple steps. Major goals are accomplished by successfully completing several smaller goals. We can read about this in Mosiah 4:27: "And see that all these things are done in wisdom and order; for it is not requisite that a man should run faster than he has strength. And again, it is expedient that he should be diligent, that thereby he might win the prize; therefore, all things must be done in order." Place the ball into the jar and fill to within 11/2" from the top with wheat. Secure the lid. Turn the jar over and demonstrate how things are accomplished one step at a time by gently shaking the jar—with each "shake" representing the accomplishment of one small goal. Continue until the ball comes out on top—symbolizing the accomplishment of a major goal.

OVERCOMING WEAKNESSES

"If [men] humble themselves before me, and have faith in me, then will I make weak things become strong unto them." Ether 12:27

•THINGS YOU WILL NEED
A sheet of newspaper (about 12" x 18")

•EXPERIMENT
Make a paper banger by following the illustrations on page 53. Once folded, grip the banger by the two sharp corners. Flick it down quickly to make a loud bang.

•GOSPEL APPLICATION
The sheet of newspaper appears to be weak and flimsy when held up for the class to see. But Heavenly Father has promised us that if we humble ourselves and have faith, he will make our weaknesses become strengths. (Ether 12:27.) In D&C 35:13, we also learn that Heavenly Father calls upon the weak things of the world to "thrash the nations." Follow the illustrations on page 53 to fold the newspaper into a paper banger. Grip the banger by the two sharp corners and flick it down sharply—demonstrating the strength and power of the once weak newspaper.

HOW TO MAKE A PAPER BANGER

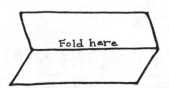

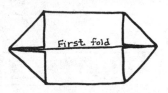

1. Fold the paper in half lengthways. Then open it out.

2. Fold each corner into the first fold.

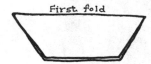

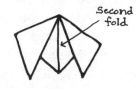

3. Fold the paper in half along the first fold. Fold it in half again.

4. Open out the second fold.

5. Fold the two outside corners down.

6. Fold the paper back along the second fold to make a triangle shape.

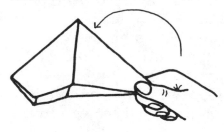

7. Grip the banger by the sharp corners. Flick it down quickly to make a loud bang.

PROTECTION FROM SIN

"But thou, O Lord, art a shield for me; my glory, and the
lifter up of mine head." Psalm 3:3

•THINGS YOU WILL NEED
One hard-boiled egg
White crayon
One cup of white vinegar
   with food coloring added

•EXPERIMENT
Using the crayon, draw and color in the shape of a
shield on the egg. Place the egg in the colored
vinegar and let sit for a minute or so. When the
egg is removed, the egg will be colored except for
the area drawn with crayon.

•GOSPEL APPLICATION
In Proverbs 30:5 it states, "Every word of God is
pure: he is a shield unto them that put their trust
in him." The egg represents an individual, the
crayon represents the word of God, and the
colored vinegar represents sin. By following the
commandments of God, we can be protected from
sin just as the crayon protected the egg from the
coloring.

54

PUTTING GOD FIRST

"Seek ye first the kingdom of God, and his righteousness; and all these things shall be added unto you." Matthew 6:33

•THINGS YOU WILL NEED
Clear glass jar
Several small balls
Dry beans
Rice
Sugar
Small sealable plastic bags

•EXPERIMENT
The various items, when placed in the jar in the proper order, fill the jar perfectly. If items are placed in the wrong order, they won't all fit.

•GOSPEL APPLICATION
Prior to the experiment, place the various items individually into small plastic bags. Label the bag of balls PRAYER.   Label the bag of beans SCRIPTURE STUDY. Label the other bags with various things such as work, hobbies, recreation, etc. Begin the experiment by placing the plastic bags labeled work, hobbies, etc., into the jar first with the bags labeled scriptures and prayers last. Unfortunately, there won't be enough room for scriptures and prayers. In Matthew 6:33 it states, "But seek ye first the kingdom of God, and his

righteousness; and all these things shall be added unto you." If we put God first in our lives by having daily prayer and scripture study, then we will have adequate time to accomplish our other desires. Demonstrate this by emptying the balls from the plastic bag into the jar. Next, empty the bag of beans (prayer) into the jar. Empty the bag of rice, then sugar into the jar until everything fits perfectly. **Note:** In order to fill the jar exactly, you may want to experiment prior to the presentation so that you can determine the proper amount needed for each item.

• ADDITIONAL APPLICATIONS

Spiritual feast—Matthew 5:6 says, "Blessed are they which do hunger and thirst after righteousness: for they shall be filled." We quench our hunger and thirst for righteousness by feasting upon spiritual things. In this experiment the bag of balls could be labeled PRAYER, the bag of beans could be labeled SCRIPTURE STUDY, the bag of rice could be labeled CHURCH ATTEND-ANCE, and the bag of sugar could be labeled SERVICE TO OTHERS. Empty the contents of the bags into the jar one at a time (starting with the largest items and ending with the smallest). After each addition it may appear there is no room left in the jar, but as each item is added, there continues to be room for spiritual food.

56

REPELLING SIN

"Submit yourselves therefore to God. Resist the devil,
and he will flee from you." James 4:7

•THINGS YOU WILL NEED
Bowl of water
Pepper
Small soap (preferably heart-shaped)
Teaspoon of sugar

•EXPERIMENT
Sprinkle some pepper into the bowl of water. Dipping the soap into the water will repel the pepper. Sprinkling the sugar into the water will attract the pepper.

•GOSPEL APPLICATION
In this experiment, the pepper represents sin, the sugar represents unrighteous living, and the soap represents righteous living. Sprinkle the pepper into the water—representing sin and unrighteousness. If we make righteous choices and have a pure heart, we will then repel sin. As stated in James 4:7, "Submit yourselves therefore to God. Resist the devil, and he will flee from you." Demonstrate this principle by dipping the soap into the water and watching the pepper flee to the sides of the bowl. When the sugar is sprinkled onto the water, the pepper is drawn toward the

sugar. Explain that unrighteous living and choices will attract sin. Place the soap into the water once again so that you end the experiment with the sin "fleeing" from you.

•ADDITIONAL APPLICATIONS

Kind words—In Proverbs 15:1 it says, "A soft answer turneth away wrath: but grievous words stir up anger." Perform the experiment as stated on the previous page with the soap representing the harshness of grievous words, the sugar representing the sweetness of kind words, and the pepper representing those around us. When we use grievous words, people around us want to flee. When we use kind words, people are drawn to us.

Repentance—In Ezekiel 18:30 we are counseled to "Repent, and turn yourselves from all your trangressions; so iniquity shall not be your ruin." The pepper represents sin (or mistakes) while the soap represents repentance. When we repent, we turn away from our sins and become clean again. Demonstrate this by placing the soap into the water. Sometimes after we repent, we make mistakes again. Demonstrate this by sprinkling the sugar onto the surface of the water. As the pepper (mistakes) return, ask the class how often they can repent and be forgiven. To find the answer, have someone read Moroni 6:8 aloud. Place the soap into the water once again and watch as the sin is turned away and the person is cleansed once again.

RESISTING TEMPTATION

"Be faithful, and yield to no temptation." D&C 9:13

•THINGS YOU WILL NEED
Paintbrush
Iodine
Small jar with water
Small bowl
Lemon (or lemon juice)
White paper

•EXPERIMENT
Squeeze some lemon juice into the bowl. Using the paintbrush, write "let us resist evil" (Alma 61:14) in lemon juice on the paper. If desired, draw in lemon juice a simple crown at the bottom of the paper. Let the lemon juice dry. Place a few drops of iodine into the jar of water. Brush the paper with the iodine mixture. The paper will turn purple, while the scripture message stays white.

•GOSPEL APPLICATION
Moroni warns us to "be wise...that ye will yield to no temptation" (Mormon 9:28). We also learn in 1 Corinthians 10:13 that "[God] will not suffer you to be tempted above that ye are able; but will with the temptation also make a way to escape, that ye

may be able to bear it." How do we escape temptation? The answer can be found in 1 Nephi 15:24: "Whoso would hearken unto the word of God, and would hold fast unto it, they would never perish; neither could the temptations and the fiery darts of the adversary overpower them unto blindness, to lead them away to destruction." Alma's counsel to his son, Helaman, teaches us to have faith in Christ, to be humble, meek, and lowly in heart, to never be weary of good works, to learn wisdom in our youth and keep the commandments of God. We should counsel with the Lord in all our doings and pray to him always. By doing all these things, we will have the strength we need to resist the temptations that surround us. (Alma 37:33-37.) Brush the iodine onto the paper, explaining that the paper represents us, and the iodine represents temptation. By resisting temptation, we will receive the blessing found in James 1:12: "Blessed is the man that endureth temptation: for when he is tried, he shall receive the crown of life, which the Lord hath promised to them that love him."

•ADDITIONAL APPLICATIONS

Keep the Sabbath day holy—Prior to class, write the words "keep thyself unspotted from the world" in lemon juice on the paper. Let the lemon juice dry. With the class, discuss various ways to keep the Sabbath day holy by referring to D&C 59:10-13. As you brush the iodine onto the paper, have someone read D&C 59:9 aloud. The iodine represents wordly influences. The white writing represents our commitment to keeping the Sabbath day holy—we are unspotted from the world. By honoring the Sabbath, the Lord has promised us both temporal and spiritual blessings (refer to D&C 59:14-19). In contrast, you could brush some iodine onto paper that has not been previously written on with lemon juice. This could represent someone who is not keeping the commandments of the Lord and is spiritually blinded by the influences of the world.

SATAN DECEIVES

"And he became Satan...the father of all lies, to deceive and to blind men, and to lead them captive at his will." Moses 4:4

•THINGS YOU WILL NEED
Newspaper
12" ruler

•EXPERIMENT
Place the ruler at the edge of a table and let it overhang about 5 inches. Unfold a single sheet of newspaper and lay it over the section of the ruler that is on the table. Bring your fist sharply down onto the free end of the ruler. The air pressure on the newspaper will resist the blow made with your fist. It might even snap the ruler in half without tearing the newspaper.

•GOSPEL APPLICATION
This experiment looks deceiving. How can the newspaper hold the ruler down, allowing it to be snapped in two? Most people would believe that the newspaper would tear before the ruler was snapped. This is similar to the way Satan works his deceitfulness. A description of Satan is found in Moses 4:4: "And he became Satan, yea, even the devil, the father of all lies, to deceive and to blind men, and to lead them captive at his will, even as many as would not hearken unto my

voice." Nephi warns us in 2 Nephi 28:7-8 that "there shall be many which shall say: Eat, drink, and be merry, for tomorrow we die; and it shall be well with us." He also warns that many will justify committing a little sin, to lie a little and take advantage of others—with the belief that God will only beat them "with a few stripes," and then they will be saved in the kingdom of God. This is exactly what Satan wants us to believe. We need to be aware of the devastating effects of sin. 1 John 1:8 warns, "If we say that we have no sin, we deceive ourselves, and the truth is not in us." Demonstrate this by using the ruler to represent an individual and the newspaper to represent their sins. The sins may not look as if they are holding the individual down, but in reality they are. Prove it by sharply striking the free end of the ruler with your fist. The ruler should resist your blow, or even break in half without tearing the newspaper.

SOFT ANSWERS

"A soft answer turneth away wrath: but grievous words
stir up anger." Proverbs 15:1

•THINGS YOU WILL NEED
Balloon

•EXPERIMENT
Blow air into the balloon. Allow the air to escape
quietly by holding the neck of the balloon gently
as the air is released. Blow air into the balloon
again. Allow the air to escape loudly by stretching
the neck of the balloon as the air is released.
Practice this beforehand to get the greatest effect.

•GOSPEL APPLICATION
In Proverbs 15:1 it says, "A soft answer turneth
away wrath: but grievous words stir up anger."
Are the answers (and words) we give soft, like the
air gently escaping from the balloon? Or are they
grievous, like the air being released loudly from
the balloon? We should always try to make our
words soft and gentle when communicating with
others.

•ADDITIONAL APPLICATIONS

Pride—The Book of Mormon is full of warnings about the danger of being puffed up in pride. Pride was always the underlying cause for destruction among the Nephites. Blow air into the balloon a little at a time as you discuss the prideful ways of the world. Continue until the balloon is so "puffed up" that it pops and is destroyed.

SPIRITUAL GIFTS

"There are many gifts, and to every man is given a gift
by the Spirit of God." D&C 46:11

•THINGS YOU WILL NEED
Scissors
Clear blue, yellow, and red plastic sheets
A white surface

•EXPERIMENT
Cut each of the clear colored sheets into several strips of equal widths. When the strips are placed onto the white surface individually, they only reflect their individual color. When the strips overlap each other, they create new colors.

•GOSPEL APPLICATION
In D&C 46:11-12, we learn the following facts about spiritual gifts: that there are many gifts of the Spirit given to man; not every gift is given to every man; each man is given at least one gift; and that these gifts are given so that "all may be profited thereby." Invite three people to come forward. Give the red strips to one person, the yellow strips to another, and the blue strips to the last. Explain that these strips are symbolic of spiritual gifts. Ask the volunteers to place their set of strips in individual piles on the white surface. If these gifts continue to lie dormant,

they profit no one. Now ask the individuals to take turns placing their strips on the white surface, letting some strips overlap at 90° angles—forming a pattern of squares (see illustration below). As the strips overlap, they create new colors, providing diversity and beauty. This is the same with our spiritual gifts. If we use them properly, others will benefit from the diversity and beauty of the various gifts that are available to each of Heavenly Father's children.

•ADDITIONAL APPLICATIONS

Talents—Each of us has been blessed with individual talents or gifts. We learn from Moroni 10:18 that these "good" gifts come from Christ. We need to use and improve these talents so that we will be given more. (D&C 82:18.) Demonstrate this by giving an individual three "talents" (a stack of blue, a stack of yellow, and a stack of red strips). Invite the person to lay the strips on the white surface as illustrated below. As the strips overlap each other, they create new colors—symbolic of new talents we can discover when we use the talents we have been blessed with. The scriptures also warn us that we can lose our God-given talents if we don't use them. (D&C 60:2-3.)

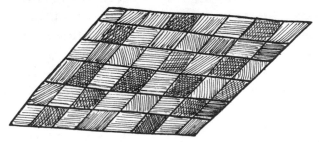

(SPIRITUAL NOURISHMENT)

"That they might be remembered and nourished by the good word
of God, to keep them in the right way." Moroni 6:4

•THINGS YOU WILL NEED
Large bowl of water
Sponge

•EXPERIMENT
Dip the sponge into the water. Hold the sponge
over the bowl and squeeze the water from the
sponge a little at a time. Refer to the lesson for
further instructions.

•GOSPEL APPLICATION
When preaching the Sermon on the Mount, Jesus
taught "Blessed are they which do hunger and
thirst after righteousness: for they shall be filled"
(Matthew 5:6). Attending church services each
Sunday is one way to quench our thirst for
righteousness. (Dip the sponge into the water.)
As we go about our week, various things will put
a drain on our spirituality. (Squeeze the sponge a
little at a time as you discuss things that might
drain our spirituality.) If we do nothing about
replenishing our spirituality during the week, we
could be completely drained by the following
Sunday—when we once again have the
opportunity to replenish our spiritual reservoir.

But, if we truly "hunger and thirst after righteousness," we will counteract the things that drain us by replenishing our spiritual reservoirs during the week. Discuss as a class various things that could replenish us, such as scripture study, prayer, service to others, etc. With the sponge, alternate squeezing a little and dipping a little to symbolize the draining and replenishing that occurs during the week. By always replenishing our spiritual reservoir, we will maintain a healthy level of spirituality and not be left completely drained come Sunday.

•ADDITIONAL APPLICATIONS

Parental responsibility—For this experiment you will need one bowl of clear water, one bowl of dark-colored water, and two light-colored sponges. As parents, we have been commanded to bring up our children in light and truth. (D&C 93:40.) Children learn by example and soak up everything—similar to a sponge. Dip the sponge into the clear water. This represents a child soaking up examples of truth and light. Jacob warned the Nephites that the bad example they set might bring destruction to their children, and they would be held accountable for the sins of their children. (Jacob 3:10.) If we set a bad example for our children, we will likewise be held accountable for their sins. Dip the sponge into the darkened water. This represents a child soaking up the bad example set by parents. We should all strive to set examples of truth and light to assure our children the best chance possible to return to live with Heavenly Father.

69

SPREADING THE GOSPEL

"Go ye into all the world, and preach the gospel to
every creature." Mark 16:15

•THINGS YOU WILL NEED
Milk (not skim)
Bowl or saucer
Food coloring
Toothpick
Liquid dish soap

•EXPERIMENT
Pour the milk into the bowl or saucer. Carefully
place a few drops of food coloring into the milk.
Do not stir. Dip the toothpick into the liquid soap,
then into the drops of food coloring. The food
coloring will spread out to the sides of the
container.

•GOSPEL APPLICATION
Proclaiming the gospel is part of the three-fold
mission of the Church. After his resurrection,
Christ taught his apostles to "Go ye into all the
world, and preach the gospel to every creature"
(Mark 16:15). We also need to do our part in
spreading the gospel. The food coloring dropped
into the milk represents the gospel. When the
toothpick is dipped in soap and then dipped into
the drops of food coloring, this represents those

individuals who are willing to share their testimony with others. Just as the food coloring spreads throughout the milk, the gospel is spread throughout the world by those willing to share.

•ADDITIONAL APPLICATIONS

Gossiping—In D&C 42:27, we are commanded not to speak evil of our neighbor. The scriptures are full of warnings against gossiping, backbiting, malice, and slander. When we spread a rumor about someone, there is really no way to correct the damage that has been done. We can say that we are sorry and ask for forgiveness, but the story has still been told, the damage is still there. This is demonstrated by the way the food coloring (stories) is spread throughout the milk by the soap-covered toothpick (a person who gossips). There is no way to reverse the process and have the food coloring return to the way it was—just as a story, once told, cannot be retrieved again.

STAY CLOSE TO THE GOSPEL

"Whoso would hearken unto the word of God, and would hold fast
unto it, they would never perish." 1 Nephi 15:24

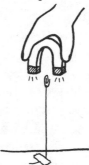

•THINGS YOU WILL NEED
Paper clip
Strong magnet
A piece of thread
Tape

•EXPERIMENT
Tie one end of the thread to the paper clip. Tape
the other end to the table. Lift the clip with the
magnet. If the magnet is pulled away too far, the
clip will fall.

•GOSPEL APPLICATION
In this experiment, man is represented by the
paper clip and the gospel is represented by the
magnet. When we live close to the gospel by
obedience to the commandments of God, we are
supported. But if we stray too far, we fall. We are
warned in Proverbs 11:14 that "Where no counsel
is, the people fall." We also learn in 1 Corinthians
10:12 that no matter who a man is and what level
he is in the gospel, he should "take heed lest he
fall." It is critical that we stay close to the gospel
teachings so that we can be supported and
strengthened in our journey to exaltation.

•ADDITIONAL APPLICATIONS

Beware of pride—Alma counsels his son, Shiblon, in Alma 38:11 not to be lifted up in pride or boast of his own wisdom and strength. Many times throughout the history of the Book of Mormon, the downfall of the people can be attributed to pride. The Lord promises in 2 Nephi 12:12 that the day will come when the "proud and lofty," and all who are lifted up "shall be brought low." Demonstrate this by having the paper clip represent man and the magnet represent pride. The more the "pride" is raised, the higher the "man" is lifted. Eventually the pride will become so "lifted up" that the man will fall and be humbled. We understand the importance of humility by reading 2 Nephi 9:42, which states: "And whoso knocketh, to him will he open; and the wise, and the learned, and they that are rich, who are puffed up because of their learning, and their wisdom, and their riches—yea, they are they whom he despiseth; and save they shall cast these things away, and consider themselves fools before God, and come down in the depths of humility, he will not open unto them."

STRENGTH THROUGH TRIALS

"Ye receive no witness until after the trial of your faith."
Ether 12:6

•THINGS YOU WILL NEED
Paper
Paper airplane-folding book (optional)

•EXPERIMENT
Fold the paper into your favorite paper airplane as you give the lesson.

•GOSPEL APPLICATION
"My people must be tried in all things," declares the Lord, "that they may be prepared to receive the glory that I have for them, even the glory of Zion; and he that will not bear chastisement is not worthy of my kingdom" (D&C 136:31). Facing trials and afflictions is one way the Lord strengthens us and helps us to prepare to receive his glory. Fold the paper into an airplane, with each fold representing a trial. You may even share a personal trial that has given you strength. Joseph Smith endured many trials throughout his life. While being held in the jail at Liberty, Missouri, he received these words of encouragement from the Lord: "My son, peace be unto thy soul; thine adversity and thine afflictions shall be but a small moment; And

then, if thou endure it well, God shall exalt thee on high; thou shalt triumph over all thy foes." Fly the airplane across the classroom to show that by enduring the "trials" (folds) the paper was given the strength needed to perform well.

STRENGTH TO ENDURE TRIALS

"The Lord will give strength unto his people." Psalm 29:11

•THINGS YOU WILL NEED
Five uncooked eggs
Clay
Several books
Plastic bag (large enough to
cover one of the books)
Bowl

•EXPERIMENT
Place the wide ends of four eggs upright into the
clay, forming a square. If necessary, the extra egg
can be broken into the bowl to prove to the class
that the eggs are raw. Place the plastic bag over
one of the books in case the eggs accidently break
during the experiment. Stack the books one at a
time on the four eggs until you have an
impressive stack. Even though the eggs appear to
be fragile, their shape makes them very strong.

•GOSPEL APPLICATION
In Mosiah 24:8-22 we can read about the people of
Alma who were in bondage to Amulon, king of
the Lamanites. During this time of great
affliction, the people cried to the Lord for
deliverance. The Lord did visit them in their

76

afflictions and caused that their burdens should be light. They were strengthened and "did submit cheerfully and with patience to all the will of the Lord" (verse 15). In Psalm 29:11, the Lord promises to bless us with strength and peace. Demonstrate this by bringing attention to the stack of books and the fragile eggs. It may seem an impossible feat to stack the books on top of the eggs without breaking them, but by carefully placing the books (starting with the plastic-covered book) one at a time on top of the eggs, it can be done. We, too, can be strengthened in our trials if we put our trust in the Lord.

•ADDITIONAL APPLICATIONS

Sharing burdens—When we are baptized, we covenant, among other things, to share one another's burdens. (Mosiah 18:8.) Begin by placing only one egg on its side in the clay. As you stack the books (burdens) on top of the egg, it will eventually break under the weight of the books. Now place four eggs in the clay, each with the wide end down. The four eggs will be able to withstand greater weight as the books are stacked on top of them. When we support each other, we are strengthened and are able to handle a greater load.

TRIBULATIONS

"Whosoever shall put their trust in God shall be supported in their trials...and shall be lifted up at the last day." Alma 36:3

•THINGS YOU WILL NEED
Small clear jar with a lid
2 tsp. metallic glitter
2 Tbs. sand
1 cup water
2 Tbs. oil

•EXPERIMENT
Place the glitter and the sand into the jar. Add the water and the oil. Screw the lid tightly onto the jar and shake vigorously. Let everything settle. The glitter will float to the top of the water, while the sand settles to the bottom.

•GOSPEL APPLICATION
As you shake the jar vigorously to represent trials, troubles, and afflictions, have someone read Alma 36:3. We learn from this verse that if we put our trust in God, we will be supported in our afflictions and be lifted up at the last day. After shaking the jar, set it down to demonstrate how the faithful (glitter) will be lifted up to receive glory, while the unfaithful (sand) will sink to the bottom. (See also D&C 58:2-4.)

•ADDITIONAL APPLICATIONS

Faith—After placing the glitter, sand, water, and oil in the jar, screw the lid on securely and hold it up for the class to see. Tell the class that you will now separate the sand from the glitter without removing the lid and without using any special tools. Ask if anyone believes that your claim is possible. Many will probably not believe, but encourage them to have faith, and not dispute your claim. Have someone read Ether 12:6. Explain that many times, our faith will be tried and tested before we receive a witness (or an answer). Begin to shake the jar vigorously to symbolize the "trial of your faith." Set the jar on a table to demonstrate how the glitter separates from the sand—providing the "witness" for your claim.

WELCOME OTHERS

"The stranger that dwelleth with you...thou shalt love
him as thyself." Leviticus 19:34

•THINGS YOU WILL NEED
Two bar magnets
Masking tape
Permanent ink marker
Stiff paper (optional)

•EXPERIMENT
Prior to the experiment, place a piece of masking
tape on each magnet. (Or, cut two small people
from stiff paper and attach one to each magnet.)
Label one magnet "ME," and the other magnet
"NEW MEMBER." Place the magnets on a flat
surface. When brought close together, the two
magnets will either attract or repel each
other—depending on which ends of the magnets
are brought together.

•GOSPEL APPLICATION
When new members or visitors attend our
church meetings, we need to do our part in
making them feel welcome. Mention several
things that a new member or visitor could
experience when they come to a meeting. If the
experience makes a person feel welcome, place the
magnets in a way where they attract each other. If

80

the experience mentioned would repel a person, place the magnets in a way where they repel each other. Encourage the class members to always make others feel welcome through their words and actions.

• ADDITIONAL APPLICATIONS

Attracting or repelling sin—Label one magnet "ME," and the other magnet "SIN." Do our thoughts, words, and actions attract or repel sin? Discuss with the class various situations that would attract or repel sin. As each is discussed, place the magnets in position so that they either attract or repel each other (depending on the situation discussed). The scriptures teach us that we should avoid even the very appearance of evil. (1 Thes. 5:22.) By doing so, we will repel sin and live a life that is worthy of blessings from our Heavenly Father.

Example—Label one magnet "MY EXAMPLE," and the other magnet "NONMEMBER." When we are baptized we promise to take upon us the name of Christ and follow the perfect example he set for us. Nonmembers will judge the Church according to the example we set. In Alma 39:11, Corianton's bad example kept the Zoramites from receiving the word of God when taught by Alma. Do our examples bring our friends closer to the Church, or do they push them away? Discuss possible situations that would either attract or discourage nonmembers from receiving the truth. Position the magnets accordingly as you discuss each situation.

ZEAL FOR RIGHTEOUSNESS

"But it is good to be zealously affected always in a good thing."
Galations 4:18

•THINGS YOU WILL NEED
Scissors
Stiff paper
Pen
Balloon
Woolen cloth

•EXPERIMENT
Cut several people from the stiff paper using the pattern above as a guide. Lay the paper people on a table. Rub the balloon on the woolen cloth, then hold the balloon about 4" above the paper people. They should jump up and down.

•GOSPEL APPLICATION
We learn in D&C 58:27 that "men should be anxiously engaged in a good cause, and do many things of their own free will, and bring to pass much righteousness." When we perform service or magnify our callings with enthusiasm, it can rub off on others. Our zeal for righteousness should show in everything we do. No matter what the activity, our positive attitude can help others get excited and involved. Demonstrate this by rubbing the balloon with the woolen cloth and

holding it over the paper people to get them "excited."

•ADDITIONAL APPLICATIONS

Missionary work—When Alma and Amulek went forth to preach the gospel, they were well received because "the Lord did pour out his Spirit on all the face of the land to prepare the minds of the children of men, or to prepare their hearts to receive the word" (Alma 16:16). If we go forth to teach our friends the gospel without preparing them first through sincere fellowshipping, they may not receive the gospel message very well. Demonstrate this by holding the balloon over the paper people before you rub it with the woolen cloth. Nothing happens. If we do our part and learn how to "rub" our friends in the right way and prepare them, they will be much more excited about the gospel message. Demonstrate this by rubbing the balloon with the woolen cloth and holding the balloon over the paper people. They should be more "enthusiastic" now.

Activation—This is performed the same way as missionary work mentioned above—only we need to learn how to "rub" the less-actives that we are responsible for in the right way so that they will once again become excited about the gospel.

INDEX

-A-

Activation, 83
Adversary, shun the, 11
    deceives, 62
Appearance, outward, 48
Armor, of God, 1
Atonement, The, 6

-B-

Balance, even, 19
Baptism, 8
    commitments, 26
Bodies, are temples, 46
Burdens, bear one another's, 10, 77
    bear up your, 13
    strength to endure, 76
Brethren, strengthen thy, 27

-C-

Callings, magnifying, 45
Children, parents' responsibility to, 69
Christ, atonement of, 6
    cleansed through the blood of, 29
    second coming of, 36
Clean living, 9
Cleansed, through repentance, 15
    through the blood of Christ, 29

86

OTHER BOOKS BY SUSAN LUKE

SUPER SUNDAYS!

Games, puzzles, service projects, music, and more are included in this treasure trove of Sabbath activities. From creating an Articles of Faith mobile, to performing a puppet show using scripture characters, to playing Book of Mormon Dominoes or Gospel Bingo, these activities are fun, interesting, varied, simple to do, and help teach important gospel principles. Best of all, they can be done reverently in keeping with the spirit of the Sabbath.

LITTLE TALKS FOR LITTLE PEOPLE

Includes text and visual aids for a dozen brief talks that children can learn quickly and enjoy presenting. Subjects like: "Love Everyone," "A Happy Home," "Noah and His Ark," "Wiggles," "Let Your Light Shine," and seven more. Short sentences make them excellent for very young children. Simple, thorough instructions show a child exactly how to prepare the visual aids and give presentations.

MORE LITTLE TALKS FOR LITTLE PEOPLE

This volume provides text and visual aids for a baker's dozen brief talks that children can learn quickly and enjoy presenting. Subjects include "My Testimony," "Daniel and the Lion's Den," "Prayer," "Songs of the Heart," "Tithing," "The True Meaning of Christmas," and seven more. These talks are so simple that an older child can easily help a younger brother or sister to prepare and present them. Both the "big people" and "little people" in your family will enjoy them for years to come!

FANTASTIC FAMILY NIGHTS!

Here's a book that has everything you need to quickly plan effective, fun, creative family nights. This book includes ideas for games, activities, lessons, charts, and visual aids. You will find a wealth of resources that will help you fulfil your responsibility to your family without having to spend undue amounts of time in preparation.

AWESOME FAMILY NIGHTS

Here's help to make family home evening the week's biggest attraction! Thirteen lessons teach children important gospel principles in fun, interesting ways; and the book includes excellent ideas for a variety of games, activities, charts, visual aids, and even refreshments.

POSITIVELY PRIMARY

If you're a Primary leader or teacher, you need this book! In these pages you'll find a wealth of simple, clever, workable ideas that you can use to make your Primary meetings more colorful, efficient, fun, and inviting. From ribbons and certificates for special recognition, to lively classroom and seating markers, to "Wow! What a Class" posters, to Primary newsletters, journals, and "Clutter Control" badges, you'll have the tools you need to make even the most ordinary Primary something extraordinary!